CRAPPIE FISHING

How to catch more and bigger crappies

© Copyright 2021 Steve Pease - All rights reserved.

It is not legal to reproduce, duplicate, or transmit any part of this document in either electronic means or in printed format.
The information provided is truthful and consistent, in that any liability, in terms of inattention or otherwise, by any usage or abuse of any policies, processes, or directions contained within is the solitary and utter responsibility of the recipient reader.

Under no circumstances can any legal responsibility or blame held against the author for any reparation, damages, or monetary loss due to the information in this document, either direct or indirect. Respective authors own all copyrights. The information in this document is for informational purposes only and is universal as so.

All trademarks and brands within this book are for clarifying purposes only and are property of the owners themselves, not affiliated with this document.

TABLE OF CONTENTS

ABOUT CRAPPIES
BEFORE YOU GO TO THE LAKE
SEASONAL
TACKLE
LIVE BAIT
LURES
RIVER FISHING
SPECIAL TECHNIQUES
ICE FISHING
EATING CRAPPIES
CONCLUSION

WHY CRAPPIES

Crappies are the most popular freshwater game fish in America. There are several reasons they are the most favored. If you fish, and you prefer to eat fish, the crappie is king. Walleyes, salmon, and trout are each good to eat, but none better than crappies.

- You can catch them throughout the year
- You can take them from most rivers and lakes around the country
- With good natural reproduction, they sustain healthy populations on their own
- They are a schooling fish, so if you get one, you can get several
- Limits on them are high enough to get a good meal every time you fish for them
- Finally, they are in the top three best eating freshwater fish you can get.

In this book we will cover all you should know related to fishing for crappies. You will learn how to take full advantage of the time you have to go fishing. I am a bass fisherman much of the time, but when I want fish to eat, I go for crappies. If you wish to have fun and catch a great fish that give you a superb meal the crappies are the king. Learn the tips I have put together to help you catch more and bigger crappies.

The best states for catching crappies are Minnesota, South Dakota, Nebraska, Kansas, Oklahoma. Also, Missouri, Illinois, Arkansas, Louisiana, Mississippi, Alabama, Tennessee, Kentucky, Virginia, and Florida are incredibly good.

These are not the only states where they are, but these are the best states for crappies.

I live in Minnesota where Crappies exist in most of our fishing lakes. Certain lakes are better than others. I will show you how to pick a good lake.

I have assembled this text to provide you a condensed book loaded with tips and techniques. It is of a length you can read over and over, so the tips are fresh in your mind every day you fish.

When you complete the book, you will know the best tips and the best way to catch more crappies.

I have been a fisherman since the mid-1960s. I have fished for many types of fish over the seasons. My favorite fishing is for bass, pike, and crappies. If I want to fish for fun, all three are fun. Crappies are a blast on ultra-light tackle. If I want to go for a meal, I fish for crappies. Although pike are also good eating.

I have caught crappies in lakes and rivers. When I was a kid, we lived on a river that had an excellent population of crappies. I caught hundreds of crappies from that river. Most of the fish I took, I caught on small inline spinners. Most of them caught from the down current side of bridge pilings. White or yellow were the strongest colors in that river. Those colors are still the best most of the time, in rivers and lakes.

I have read every book and article I have found on crappie fishing to learn the best tips and techniques. I have an abundance of knowledge to share and help you boost your fishing skills.

After you read this book, you will recognize the best places to search for crappies and catch them. If you put these tips and techniques to use, you will get more fish when you go fishing. The book is a quick study and a refresher to learn and put the tips fresh in your mind when you hit the lake.

Grab your copy now and be a better crappie fisherman today. Get it now on Amazon.

ABOUT CRAPPIES

One of the most important concepts to learn about crappie fishing is they have a soft mouth. When setting the hook for any crappie fishing, you need to use a sweeping hook set. You cannot set the hook like you do for bass, or even sunfish, or you will rip the lure or bait through their lip. Remember this one tip and you will land more fish.

It is hard to do a sweeping hook set if you are not used to it. When you fish for bluegills and the bobber goes down, you snap set the hook hard and you will hook them. If you do that with crappies, you will not hook them. It takes getting used to and keeping that fresh in your mind.

There are two types of crappies, black and white. The techniques needed to catch them are identical. They even taste the same. Many people do not realize there is a distinction between them. Most crappie fishermen are not particular about which ones they are catching. Some crappie waters contain both blacks and whites. There are most often more of one type in a specific body of water.

Black crappies prefer large slow-flowing rivers and cool, clear lakes. Black crappies most of the time are darker than white crappies. The whites have the spots on their sides in regular vertical bars. The black crappies spots are more random. The difference is not enough to judge by color only.

The best way to tell the difference between blacks and whites is by looking at the dorsal fin. Black crappies most often contain seven or eight spines. White crappies six. I would not worry much about which one you are catching.

The average lifespan for crappies is 10 years in the wild. They can survive longer in captivity. As with most fish, crappies grow slower in the cooler northern lakes than in warmer southern reservoirs. They grow to the same size in northern lakes, only not as fast.

Crappie size

This is the average size crappie you will catch most places.

½ pound to 1-pound crappies are the most frequent size crappies. There are many places you can catch bigger ones. The ones over a pound are slabs. Top crappie waters produce fish in the one to three-pound range, and they can get much bigger.

The Minnesota State record for black crappies is 5 pounds. The Minnesota record for whites is 3 pounds 15 ounces. The world record black is the same weight, 5 pounds. The world record white crappie is 5 pounds 3 ounces. These record fish all lived in rivers.

You can catch big crappies in lakes but if it is giants you are going for, a river is a better bet. The biggest crappies can grow up to 20 inches long.

General tips to catch more crappies

- Set the hook easy. Do not set it like you would set it with any other fish, or you will rip it out of their mouth. Use a firm sweeping motion.
- After you hook the fish, keep the line tight. Loose line gives the crappie a way to get off.
- If you are not catching fish, change the depth before switching the lure. Crappies are depth sensitive. Depth is more important than color.

- Use light wire hooks and light line.
- Most of the year, crappies are schooling fish. Do not spend a lot of time waiting for the fish to find your bait. Move if there are not fish where you are fishing.
- Make sure you have sharp hooks.
- Use thin wire hooks to allow for lighter hook set.
- If you are trolling, and you catch a fish, stop trolling and fish that spot. Crappies are schooling fish; you will find others close by.
- Do not get too close. If you find a spot, stay back. Cast to the spot so you do not spook the fish.
- If you catch bigger crappies, use a net to land them. You can rip their mouth and lose the fish from the weight of the fish hanging in the air out of the water.
- When you hook a crappie, keep the line tight. If you give them slackline, they can shake out the hook.
- Take your time when landing them. Do not get too aggressive when reeling them in.

- A cool tip when they are not biting. You need to be fishing where 2 lines are legal or have a friend fishing with you. Cast out a bobber rig with a live minnow. Have the second line with a spinner or small crankbait. Cast the lure past the bobber rig and reel it close to the bobber rig at a fast speed. You will draw fish to the bobber rig with the spinner and the crappies will take the minnow instead of passing it up.
- Slow down. Fishing slower will get you more fish.

WATER CLARITY

First, you need to determine how to gauge water clarity. If you go to the DNR website in your state and view the readings on the lake you are fishing. You can see the Secchi disk reading for the lake. If the reading is six feet or more that is clear water. A stained or colored water reading is 2 to 6 feet. If the reading is less than two feet that is muddy or dirty water.

Clear water

Water clarity will affect fishing for most fish species, crappies are no different. In Minnesota I have fished lakes from dark water where the disc is only visible a foot deep in the water. I have also fished in water where you can see 20 feet deep.

Lake Itasca, the start of the Mississippi river, is the clearest lake I have ever fished. The weed line is over 20 feet deep. It is a fantastic lake to kayak or canoe, but tough to fish because it is so clear.

Crappies are sight feeders. In clear water you want to stay far away from where you think the fish will be. Low light periods are best in shallower water. Early morning and late in the day are prime times. Cloudy days are better than clear sunny days. Night fishing in clear water can also be fantastic. A bright moon makes it even better. The silhouette of the minnow or lure against a light night sky is visual for the fish.

Minnows or small jigs with a light line is best in clear water. Minnows are great because it is all real looking to the crappie, and they love minnows. Use more natural-looking jigs, or translucent color jigs, they are best. A pearl color, a spotted minnow color, or the old standby that is always effective, white, will work best. A glitter or sparkle effect will work well by adding more flash.

Light line is also important in clear water. 4 pound is best, 6 is ok. If you use bigger line, the fish can see the line. and it makes them think it does not look natural. Not saying you cannot catch fish on a larger line, but you will not catch as many.

Stained water

Stained water is between clear and muddy. The level of difference will determine which way to focus your technique. In somewhat stained, lean toward the clear, in dark stained lean toward the muddy.

As the water clarity darkens, move toward the bright-colored jigs. The chartreuse, pinks, and bright yellows. Adding a grub, wax worm, or minnow on the jig will help in the darker water. Scent will help as the water clarity darkens.

Muddy water

In muddy water, the crappies will stay in shallower water. Low light levels in deeper water prevents good oxygen levels in deeper water. This forces the fish to stay shallower. There is a lake in New Brighton Mn that I have fished often. The water is dark stained. The Secchi disk reading is 3 ft. The water is on the low end of stained. Minnows work well, bright yellow and orange jigs have worked best for me in this lake. The nice thing about this lake is that it has a good population of crappies. And they stay in shallower water all year.

FISHING A NEW LAKE

One of the biggest ways you can improve your success when going to fish a new lake is to do your homework before you go. You will learn how much unproductive water you can rule out before you even get to the lake. Learning what is going on under the surface. How fish change, and how lakes change will keep you catching fish.

Lake Maps

One of the most important things to do before you go to the lake is get a good lake map. There are books that have maps, and there are maps of most lakes you can buy online.

One of the best options for detailed lake maps is Navionics. They have an app you can buy for your phone. It is not a cheap app, but if you fish many lakes, it is well worth it. The maps they have are much more detailed than you can get anywhere else.

If you go to their website, and scroll down to the bottom, you can see maps of lakes that show detail free. This is a great place to start.

Go to the map of the lake you will fish. Look for the points, the sharp drop-offs, underwater humps, islands, and weed lines. Crappies as most other freshwater fish are structure oriented most of the time. Structure draws small fish; crappies follow the food.

Note on your map any creeks going in or out of the lake. Highlight any bridges or other obvious structures on the lake that will attract fish.

Mark your paper map with the prime spots you find on the lake map. After that go to Google Maps and find the lake in the overhead or birds eye view. Look at the earth view so you can see the actual picture from the satellite.

While you are on this view, note where the docks are and how big they are. Docks are a key structure;

they attract lots of baitfish and thus attract a lot of crappies.

Use the cursor to get the GPS coordinates of the points that look like productive structure points to hold fish. If you have a GPS device, or have GPS on your phone. You can go to the exact place you chose from the coordinates you got from the earth view map.

If your state has a DNR website like Minnesota. Go to that site to find out more useful information on the lake. [The Minnesota lake finder site](#) has lots of other good information. You see water clarity, what species of fish are prevalent in the lake, if they stock it and when and what they stocked. You can also see DNR sampling to see how many of what fish they counted. this is useful information.

The water clarity gives a depth. The lake I am looking at has averaged between 1.2 meters and 2.1 meters over the past 20 years.

Use the water clarity depth along with what you can see on Google Maps from the satellite view. With this information, you will have a good idea where the weed lines will be on the lake.

The weed lines in this lake should be around 6 feet deep. We also know the water is clear, about normal for natural lakes in this area.

The main way to find fish is to follow the food. In natural lakes, we do not have schools of baitfish swimming in deep water. Most northern bait fish stay close to or inside of structure. They also stay in shallower water than in southern reservoirs.

The food fish are structure related. Their only defense against becoming lunch is to hide from the bigger fish in and around the structure.

We can assume most of the crappies in this lake will be in less than 15 feet of water. That is where the food will be. They will hide in the weeds, or outside the edges of the weeds.

The crappies will feed in those areas because that is where the food is. Using the lake maps, Google Maps, and the DNR site, you can rule out 80% of the water on the lake. You can tell that most of the lake will not hold crappies before you even leave the computer. When the fish are active and hungry, catching them is easy if they are in the spots they should be.

Local Information

Getting local fishing information is also another great way to find the best places to fish. You can look at fishing report sites that give the weekly fishing report from lakes in the area.

If you look in your area, you will find useful information about recent fish catches. You will also find what depth and cover they are in.

If you have a cabin on a lake, or a lake you fish a lot, the lake association meetings are a wealth of information on your lake.

There is a great site that started in Minnesota Outdoor news. They have fishing reports from several other Northern states and Minnesota.

There are also sites like Lake State fishing. This site gets updated by resorts that want people to know where and what fish are active that week. Look for these types of sites in your area.

Another great way to get local information is to call local bait shops. When you call them, do not ask where they are biting. You will get a better response if you ask things that are to confirm what you have already determined.

Such as, are the crappies hitting off the deep point in the center of the lake still? Or have they moved into the shallower grass and weed beds at the south end of the lake. etc. Try confirming what you have determined in your research.

You can also search Google by typing in the lake name followed by fishing reports. You will pull up information on fishing reports. You will also get information from any fishing tournaments that have taken place on the lake. This is valuable information to know.

The fishing report search will get information from local guides and resorts. These people want you to know where the fish are active. They want to get you to come to their lake. Look through these reports. Read reviews from people that stayed at the resorts or used the guides.

This is a great confidence builder. You can see you figured the lake out without even fishing it yet.

Make a plan

Once you gather all this information and mark out the most likely places to be productive on your map. Then you are ready to make a plan of attack to fish the lake.

The plan is the key to success on a new lake; do not skip this part if you want to catch lots of fish. When you make your plan, always fish the structure you determine, at the shallowest points. Start shallow and work your way deeper. Shallow fish are more active and easier to catch.

SEASONAL

One of the best things about crappies is that you can take them year-round. There are differences in the various seasons. Check the laws where you live on the seasons and limits. I live in Minnesota where the season never closes for crappies. The daily limit is 10 fish.

SPRING

Spring is when crappie fishing can be the hottest and most fun. When the fish move into the shallows to spawn, fishing can be fantastic. You can catch a limit of fish in a matter of minutes. Crappies spawn in the 60-to-65-degree range. With water temps below they will be shallow and catchable.

Springtime is the easiest time for crappies. After the ice goes off the lakes, the crappies move into shallow water. Warm water attracts crappies. You can catch them in a foot of water or less sometimes. The north end of the lake is best. The north end of the lake is the best place to go on those sunny spring days. The warmer wind from the south moves the warm water to the north end of the lake. The sun hits the north end for more of the daylight hours.

Docks, shallow weed beds and other underwater structures will hold crappies in the spring. My brother and I were fishing on a small lake in northern Anoka county late one spring. We were looking to catch crappies for a meal. We were in a bay on the north end of the lake where the bottom was dark, not sandy. We fished with crappie minnows and we both had our limit in half an hour.

Every cast we caught a fish. This was a few years ago. The limit was 15 fish each. Other species were not opened to catch. Our fishing was over that quick.

We went home and cleaned the fish and had a great lunch. It was a strange day. You never expect to finish fishing that quick, but it was awesome.

Depending on what part of the country you are in, spring crappie fishing gets better when the night's stay above freezing, and the ice goes off the lakes. The water warms and the crappies get the urge to find a nest and create more crappies.

The pre spawn and spawning times are the best time to find and catch crappies. They will be shallow looking for nesting areas. Crappies spawn in 60-to-65-degree water.

Before the spawn they will spend much of their time in less than ten feet of water. Looking for nesting areas and gorging themselves on food. The females need to eat for strength and to help them spawn.

Crappies in natural lakes spawn on the wind protected side of muddy or dark bottom bays. Before they move into the spawning areas, they school up on the outside edge of break lines, or any remaining weeds or stumps.

When they move into the spawning areas, the males get aggressive and will hit about anything that gets in front of them. The females will also strike if you get close to the nest, but they are much less aggressive.

They will set up their nests near cover in shallow bays. *A key point is they will nest in the same areas every year. So, if you find spring crappies in a lake, you will find them again in the same spots every year.*

Baits for spring crappies.

Live bait is the best bait for crappies in the spring. Because the crappies are in shallow water, fishing crappie minnows below a bobber is the most effective way. Because they are in shallow water, a fixed bobber is the best method to use.

Jig fishing and slow trolling and casting also work well, but live bait is the best in the spring. Casting with roadrunner jigs is another great technique.

SUMMER

In the summer, crappies spread out, this makes them harder to find. The crappies will move out to the deeper structure. In impoundments, look for flooded timber and creek channels. In northern lakes, the crappies move to deeper structure areas. Deep weeds, humps, and points. Look for schools of baitfish and you will find schools of crappies.

Tipping the jig with a minnow works like a champion. You want to use bigger jigs in the summer to get the jig deeper. Use jigs up to ¼ oz.

Vertical jigging is important in summer structure fishing. Crappies in summer are always around cover. There is a good spot on our lake that holds crappies most of the year. The spot is in 8 to 10 feet of water on the edge of a weed line. Where the weeds stop the bottom drops to 16 feet.

This spot is great, I can cast to it from our dock. Fisherman come from all over the lake to fish our spot. The spot always seems to have crappies in it all year long.

It makes my crappie fishing easy on our lake. I can catch crappies with a minnow on a hook under a bobber, but I prefer to fish them with a jig with or without a minnow. I also can catch them with a small beetle spin, an inline spinner, or a small crankbait. It gives me a lot of variety for how I can catch fish.

In the summer, live bait is by far your best bet. A jig tipped with a crappie minnow will be best. Keeping minnows in the summer is sometimes hard. I have found that keeping them in an insulated bucket with an aerator is best. I also add [sure life foam off](#) and [sure life better bait](#) to keep my minnows, alive and active in the summer.

These products seem at first to be expensive. You use little of the product. One bottle of each product will last you for years. We go fishing every weekend in the summer with live bait. I have used this product for a couple of years. These bottles will last another five years or longer.

When you are looking for crappies after they move to deeper water, there are several places you will find the best schools of fish. Any underwater brush or flooded trees are a key structure. Another key spot is break lines. Break lines are when the bottom drops. In many lakes there are break lines where the bottom drops at the weed lines.

Fishing a break line is like a weed line. The lake where I fish has sharp weed lines. The weed lines are at around six feet. The reason for the sharp weed lines in our area of the lake is because the bottom drops from six feet to 15 feet in about 30-foot space.

We have our dock set, so it is at the edge of the weed line. It makes it perfect for crappie fishing from the dock most of the year. We can cast to the weeds and at the weed line. I can even reach the drop off with ease.

Find the break lines from the shoreline. The steeper the shore, the faster the drop off and the more likely you will find a good break line.

The break line does not have to be big; a break line of a couple feet can be an attractive area for crappies. It creates an edge. Edge structure is great for many fish, including crappies.

FALL

In the fall the crappies move back into the shallows with the baitfish and the cooler water. You can find them in the same places you did in the spring around the shallow structures and weeds. They are there for different reasons now. Not to spawn, but to feed. Food and warmer water are the main concerns in the fall.

In the fall the crappies will go for bigger minnows. The baitfish have been growing all summer. The crappies are expecting bigger food. Using bigger jigs can be better for catching more fish and bigger fish.

Cast and retrieve with a jig. You can use it under a bobber or without a bobber. I like to use a fixed round bobber for this fishing. Use a bobber just big enough buoyancy to float the jig at the depth you want it to be. Smaller bobbers make the retrieve easier because of less resistance when you are slow reeling. When I say slow, I mean slow. You want it to move slow at a steady rate.

WINTER

In the winter, the crappies will seek the warmest water. The warm water will be in the deeper water, 15 to 30 feet deep in most lakes. If you know a place in the lake 15 to 30 feet deep with structure that will be the best place to fish. The shallow areas and the deep areas of the lake will not have enough oxygen.

Ice fishing for crappies has advantages over open water fishing. Crappies will school tighter and will be easier to find. They have fewer places where they can find comfort in winter. They will more often be in larger schools and suspended over deeper water.

Most of the year you will find crappies in 12 to 18 feet of water. In the spring and fall they will be shallower. They will be deeper most of the rest of the year. You can catch them up to 30 feet deep in some lakes and sometimes of the year, but 12 to 18 feet is the optimum for most lakes.

TACKLE

Using light tackle is important when crappie fishing. Many people call crappies paper mouths because of their thin mouth. A hard hook set, and you will tear their mouth and you will lose them. The technique for setting a hook with crappies differs from any other freshwater fish. You need to use a sweeping motion. Light line and a rod with a soft tip are also important in crappie fishing tackle.

Crappie rods

Almost any rod and reel combo will work for catching crappies. Some are much better than others. The best rods for crappie fishing depend on how and where you are fishing for them. When they are in shallow water in the spring, the best setup is a telescopic cane pole. They are inexpensive and easy to transport. I prefer a 12 foot one. You put the line on it that is the same length as the pole. This setup gives you a reach from where you are fishing over 20 feet.

It works so well because you can hold the pole in one hand, hold the line in the other. Then release the line and swing the bait to the exact spot you want to put it. If you do not get a bite, you lift it up and repeat. If you are using a minnow or a jig, this method works great in shallow water. It is even effective if you are shore fishing and you can get in front of the right spots.

There is a small lake in the northern twin cities that has a good population of nice crappies. No motors allowed on the lake. It is the perfect lake for this fishing. We take out the canoe with our cane poles, go to the north end of the lake. This part of the lake is a shallow area with cattails out from the shore for about 100 feet. There is no way to get close to the water from the shore. From the canoe, we can move close to the shore and drop the bait right next to the cattails.

Cattails grow in areas with a muddy bottom. That muddy bottom warms the water faster in the spring. The bigger crappies come up into the shallows in this area and you can catch crappies one after the another. These rods also work good for hook sets. They have tips that have lots of bend to them. It makes you set the hook softer. You also cannot set the hook hard with a 12-foot rod. It makes you do a sweep type set. I use this setup most of the time with a plain hook, a small split shot, and a fixed bobber. Set the bobber shallow and go to it.

You can also use this setup with a small colorful jig, by itself or tipped with a minnow if they are being finicky.

When they move into deeper water, the cane pole is not a great choice. You will want to go to a spinning or spin casting rod. I like an open face ultra-light spinning rod with a light reel and 6-pound line. I like to use mono on crappie rods because the extra stretch of the line has forgiveness if you set the hook too hard.

I do not know about you, but I still forget sometimes and set the hook hard like I would for sunfish. You will lose most Crappies if you set the hook that hard.

If the crappies have moved deeper, you cannot fish a cane pole in water that is more than about 4 feet deep. Even though you can set the bobber to let the bait go deeper, you cut the distance you can deliver the bait every foot you move the bobber up the line.

You will also need to use slip bobbers or no bobber when you get into where crappies hang out in the summer months in the deeper water.

I see guys in the south using the cane poles with ultra-light reels and fishing with many rods doing the spider rigging thing. In Minnesota we can only use one line per person, so I have never done that. I also do not care for fishing a long cane pole with a reel on it. I do not feel like I have the same control as I do with a 6 or 6 ½ foot ultralight rig.

This is my favorite crappie fishing set up. I have a Shakespeare telescopic 6ft rod. I have a bass pro underspin reel on it with 6-pound line. I can carry this set up in my tackle box, so it is available anytime I am fishing.

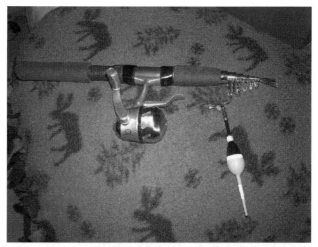

I know it does not look like much, but it is highly effective. I have caught a ton of crappies on this rig. because when I am bass fishing and I decide I want to catch crappies for a meal, I always have it with me. If I go crappie fishing, I have a Shimano ultralight rod and reel with a Shimano ultralight reel I can use.

Reels

Like I said above. The best reels are small ultralight reels spooled with 6-pound line. I use the underspin reel and I like that one. You can use spincast reels. They also work well. They have an advantage as does the underspin. The one-handed casting is an advantage. If you have not used a spin cast reel, they have gotten much better. They are not a little kid reel anymore.

There are cheap, low quality spin cast reels out there. Like any other reel. Read the reviews before you buy one and make sure it will deliver what you need.

Line

I prefer to use mono for crappies. Braided line is great, but it is not forgiving if you set the hook hard. There is no line stretch, all that energy from the hook set goes right to the hook and tears the crappies mouth.

Terminal tackle

I carry an assortment of split shot sinkers, a few bobbers, and some hooks for crappies. I use hooks a little bigger than what I use for sunfish. Crappies have a bigger mouth, and it makes it easier to get the hook through the minnow.

Simple is the best way to go for crappie fishing with live bait. I use fixed bobbers for shallow and slip bobbers when the fish are deeper. When the fish are over 6 feet deep, casting is difficult using a fixed bobber. A slip bobber will let you fish much deeper and make it easy to cast. Rigging a slip bobber is easy. Follow the directions on the package to make it work.

I also carry an assortment of small jigs. Roadrunner jigs are some of my favorite. The roadrunner jigs catch lots of crappies. They come in a variety of colors.

Many times, in the summer, Crappies are suspending in fifteen feet or deeper. You need the slip bobber to fish that deep with live bait. Jigs work with or without bobbers.
Here is one of my favorite jigs. This or the white seem to work best. Roadrunner jigs.

Fuzzy grub jigs are also great crappie jigs. They also come in many colors. Crappies like bright colors most of the time. Most any small jigs will catch crappies, these are my favorites.

Crappie jigs come in curly tail, ripple tails, they come with marabou, hair tails, tinsel tails, and many other types of material. You can get the tails in every color imaginable. They come with lead heads, floating heads standing heads and diving heads.

The best sizes for crappie jigs are 1/32 oz to ¼ oz. Most of the time you will use 1/16 and ⅛ oz. The curly tail and the tube style jigs like the fuzzy grub and the roadrunners are my favorites.

There are great combo sets of crappie jigs you can get that are great for a decent price. Here is a set from Bass Pro Shops.

There are general rules for colors for jigs. These are guidelines. Bright colors work in most any color water, but these guidelines will give you ideas for the best colors.

- In clear water use natural colors
- Bright sunny days, use yellow, white, pink, chartreuse, or combinations. Natural colors will also work.
- Dark water use the brightest colors you have.
- For cloudy days use darker colors to make a better silhouette, they will look up most of the time so it will show up easier. Also use a spinner for flash. A beetle spin or a roadrunner.

Tackle box

Any tackle box will work for crappie fishing. The way I do it is using a box in a box. I have several Plano 3600 boxes inside my tackle box. One of them I use for my crappie tackle.

I carry an assortment of split shot sinkers, a few bobbers, and some hooks. I also carry an assortment of small jigs. Roadrunner jigs are some of my favorite. The roadrunner jigs catch lots of crappies. They come in a variety of colors. I also carry an assortment of small beetle spins.

Hooks

Many fishermen think red hooks are better. Others say they do not make a difference. It is one thing that there is no way to tell. My wife is an avid live bait fisherwoman, and she swears by them. I am sure they do not hurt fishing. She uses them for all her fishing, and she catches many large pike and bass on minnows and red hooks.

The best hooks for crappies are light wire brass hooks. They are best for piercing the mouth of the crappie because they are thin and are sharp. It is also better for the minnows; you will push the hook through the minnow easier and not kill as many. The light wire hooks also have a longer shank which I also like better for crappie fishing.

#2 or #4 are the best hooks, with smaller minnows. You will catch even big crappies on the smaller hooks with no problem.

If you are fishing them under a bobber, hook them through the back, behind the dorsal fin. Go down far enough to go below the spine. If you do this right, they can live for quite a while.

The key is to get them eaten by the crappies. If I am tipping a jig or trolling, I hook them through the lips. Up from the bottom. Go through bottom and top lip.
Some guys like to hook them through the eyes. I have not done it but that would kill them much faster than through the lips.

Bobbers

I use fixed bobbers and slip bobbers, depending on the depth I am fishing. If I am fishing shallower than 4 or 5 feet, I will use a fixed bobber. Any deeper and a slip bobber is the way to go.

I like the thin pencil bobbers when fishing shallow. They have little resistance, and you can see right away when there is a crappie biting on the bait. The pencil bobber will show you more bites and you will catch more fish. I also will sometimes use a small round bobber when fishing a jig over submerged structure. If I know the fish are at a depth, I can keep the jig a foot or 2 above them.

LIVE BAIT

When considering using live bait or artificial for crappies. Many times, the best solution is to use both. For live bait, the minnow is the most used and most effective. Crappies like minnows and they like them alive. Only starving crappies will eat dead minnows.

Many fishermen think bigger minnows are better. But many lifetime crappie fishermen will tell you that one and a half inch and smaller minnows are best. Even for bigger fish.

HOOKS

The best live bait hooks are brass hooks. They are not as rigid and will bend if snagged on weeds or other structure. They are thinner so they seem to be sharper. Sharp hooks get through the mouth quick and easy. A smaller gap hook is better to keep the fish hooked. The wider the gap, the easier for the fish to throw out the hook.

Hooking them through the lips will keep them alive longer. Hooking them behind the dorsal fin makes them look more natural on a bobber rig. It makes them look injured and like an easy meal. I have observed people hooking them through the tail. I have not tried this approach, but some fishermen do.

Keep your minnows up off the bottom. Crappies will not feed on the bottom.

If you live near a pet store, feeder minnows they sell at pet stores can be excellent for crappies. They are orange or orange and white. The colored minnows can be an extra attractant for crappies.

Special tip

Chop an onion into tiny pieces. Put them in a medicine bottle and bring them with you. Hook a small piece on your hook and run the hook through the lower and upper lip of the minnow. It will get you more fish. This tip also works with jigs. Put the jig in the medicine bottle and shake it up before you use it. You will catch more fish with the jig.

Maggots are one of the best crappie live baits there is after minnows. If you can get them, use them. Wax worms are the next closest type of grub. They are much easier to get.

Advantages to using a bobber.

- Depth control is much easier
- If the fish are spooky from a cold front or no wind. You can cast to them from farther away.
- The presentation is very subtle if they are spooky
- You can keep the bait in front of them much longer
- The bobber gives you a visual show of a bite.

Slip Bobber

Using a slip bobber, the best retrieve is to cast it out and let it sit still until the ripples stop. Slow retrieve the bobber about halfway back to the boat and then reel it in for the next cast. This technique is fantastic with a jig.

There are many types of bobber stops. Most of them work ok, but the best ones I have found are these from bass pro shops. They are easy to install and stay in place. They also have them at Cabela's.

Rigging the slip bobber.

- If you use the bobber stops, I recommended, put on the bobber stop
- put on the bead
- Next comes the bobber
- the sinkers or weight, set about a foot above the hook
- Last is the hook

To change the depth you are fishing, move the bobber stop up or down the line to the depth you want to fish. It is that easy.

CRAPPIE LURES

☐Live bait and jigs work great. There are other lures you can use for crappies. Some of them are great. Beetle spins are an excellent lure for crappies. A slow retrieve with a beetle spin is effective for crappies any time of year.

The next best lures are inline spinner baits, they are great for crappies. Mepps and Rooster tail inline spinners both work well. I have taken hundreds of crappies on white and yellow rooster tail spinners, and black and yellow mepps. A slow retrieve is best anytime you are casting for crappies. They are not big on chasing fast moving lures any time of year.

Small crankbaits will catch crappies.
In southern lakes where there are schools of shad. Crankbaits are highly effective when the shad schools move into the shallow water in the fall. You will catch bigger crappies on crankbaits this time of the year, but not as many. In northern lakes crank baits are not as useful. You can take them on smaller crankbaits, but I do not think it is the best option. You will take more crappies on jigs or minnows, or jigs with minnows.

Storm Wildeye live jigs are great. They are a combination jig and realistic looking minnow. Slow retrieve with or without a bobber.

One key point to remember when fishing crappies with artificial lures is, you will catch more fish if you vary the retrieve. You can catch fish with a steady retrieve, but you will catch more fish if you change the retrieve speed. Pause for a second and start again. Another thing I do that I also do when bass fishing is move the rod tip side to side every couple of cranks. This makes the jig or spinner dart side to side and move like a real minnow would move.

Using bright colors and changing baits can be a key in triggering strikes. Color is important to crappies. Changing the color can induce a strike when the current lure is not getting hit. Try changing depth before color.

Fly-fishing for crappies
Fly-fishing can be effective for crappies. One of the great things about fly-fishing for crappies is you need not spend a lot for the equipment. A 6 1/2 to 8 ft fly rod with a low-cost reel will work for most crappie fishing.

Use a 5 ft tapered leader. Dry flies can work in some situations. In most situations for crappies, wet flies will be best. The great thing about fly-fishing for crappies is the flies drop slow in the water. You can get to the right depth slow so it will not spook the fish.

If you know the depth, the fish are at, you can keep the fly 1 to 3 feet above the school to get them to come up.

Use bright colored flies. Flies that look like a minnow or an insect will work to catch crappies. That covers most flies. Clouser minnow flies are one of the best crappie flies, and they are easy to get about anywhere. Mickey Finn flies are also great for crappies. Nymph patterns are also good.

If you want to use dry flies for crappies, fish early in the morning or at sunset with a calm lake. That is when the insects are being eaten off the surface of the water.

RIVER FISHING

☐While most crappie fishing takes place in lakes, rivers can offer fantastic crappie fishing in the spring and fall. There is a place I have taken many crappies out of the Mississippi river, just a couple miles from my home.

The place is a dam on the river in Coon Rapids Minnesota. One side of the dam has a heavy flow of water. On the East side of the dam, there is a small area that used to have water running through it. The flow has since stopped on the east side. The channel downriver from the dam on the east side is still there. It formed a backwater area about 3 to 6 feet deep. In the spring and fall the crappies come into this warm water space and you can hook one every cast.

Backwater areas in rivers can be great. Baitfish go there, and as most fish that eat other fish, where the food goes, the predators follow.

In the main river channels, look for structure or eddies. Something to break the current. Crappies will not fight the strong current, they will be in slack water areas. In slow moving water where weeds grow, do not pass up weeds in the river. Likewise, any brush or flooded stumps will hold fish.

The down-current side of rip rap and sandbars will hold fish.

In the spring, many rivers flood places that do not always contain water. This can create many slack water areas that will attract bait fish, which will attract crappies. Do not pass them up.

SPECIAL TECHNIQUES

Spider rigging

This is a technique I have not tried. I have seen it done, and it looks amazingly effective for finding fish on large bodies of water. In Minnesota where I live it is not something we can do. We can only use one rod per person fishing in the water at a time. Ice fishing you can use 2.

This technique is where you put a bunch of rods out on a bunch of rod holders. They are at different depths and baited with different lures. The lures are slow trolled until you find the fish.

They use 14-to-16-foot rods with lite line and ultra-lite reels. When you find the fish, change the lures and the depth to match where the fish are on the other rods.
Here is a video that shows you how to set it up. It looks like a lot of work, but remarkably effective.

Shore fishing for crappies

The best time for shore fishing for crappies is in the spring when they are shallow. As with anywhere else, structure is key. The best structures to look for are standing timber, brush piles, riprap, docks, and bridge pilings.

The best baits are minnows fished below a bobber, fixed or slip. Accurate casts with a 1/32 or 1/64th oz jig next to these structures will work well. The light jig will sink through the strike zone at a slow rate. A stop and go retrieve works well once you are in the strike zone near visible structure. If you are fishing riprap, a steady retrieve should work best.

Summer shore fishing.

In summer rivers are the best bet for shore fishing. Also, in the winter in places where the water does not freeze. The crappies move deeper as the water warms and often suspend in deep channels. Bridges are great because they give you access to deeper water and because they give you access to the bridge pilings.

Bridge pilings are crappie magnets in the summer and winter. They provide shade in the hot months. They also act as funnels to channel minnows and food to a part of the river, so you do not have to fish the entire river. Focus on the down current side where the fish have a place to sit in the slack area behind the piling. Earlier and later in the day, fish the shallower piling. In midday fish the deeper ones.

If you live near small lakes and ponds that have cattails around the shore, these can be fantastic. Crappies like to spawn in shallow cattails. Get a 14-to-16-foot cane pole that will let you reach out to the edge of the cattails. If you can drop a minnow at the outside edge of the cattails, you will catch crappies.

Another handy tool for shore fishing is a small depth finder you can cast out from shore to see the structure and depth. There are several of them on the market. Several of them work through an app you get on your phone, so they are inexpensive and are handy to have. They are also helpful when ice fishing.

Shooting docks

I saw a video of a guy down south doing this several years ago and I thought it was awesome. Why did I never think of that? It makes such good sense, and it works, it catches fish. I have even used it for bass, and it works great.

In northern lakes there are crappies on deeper docks most times of the year. Shooting docks is a great technique to catch crappies in northern lakes. Shooting docks is a simple technique and easy to do. I fish from a kayak most of the time, so shooting docks is easy. I am at the right level when I start.

You want to use a rod with a flexible tip. Hold the rod in your fishing hand and hold the bait with your other hand, have the jig about two feet above the bottom of the rod. Pull the jig down to bend the end of the rod. Use the bend to get spring to shoot the jig under the dock.

Open the bail and hold the line with your finger, pull down on the jig and release the jig letting the bend in the rod slingshot the jig under the dock, right to where fish are waiting. Docks that are close the water are hard to shoot, but do not pass them up. Even if you do not get under, shooting will get you right up to the dock posts where many fish like to sit.

Be ready when the jig hits the water. Many times, as it falls is when it will get bit. Keep track of the docks where you find fish. They will many times be productive docks. The reason being there is food and good cover under and around that dock.

Use the lightest jig you can. Light jigs will fall slower and keep it in front of the fish longer. Make sure you hold the jig on the sides of the hook, so you do not slip and shoot it into your finger.

Use and open faced spinning reel with a light line. [Here is a good video](#) that shows you how to do it. It takes practice to get good at this. You can even practice at home by trying to shoot your jig low to a spot. Try to be about the same level above the ground as you are above the water in your boat.

ICE FISHING FOR CRAPPIES

Crappies are active, pretty much year-round. They are active and you can catch them through the ice in the northern lakes. Finding crappies in the winter is much easier if you have the right equipment. The best things to have are a portable depth finder, a power ice auger, and an underwater camera.

You do not need a camera, but it is nice. Another important piece of equipment that is unnecessary, but useful, is a sled. You do not need a portable shelter, but it is worth the money if you want to do, serious ice fishing.

There are several manufacturers that make useful shelters and sled combos. It will make your ice fishing much easier. Clam, Otter, Frabill, Elkton, Eskimo and I am sure several others.

In the winter, the crappies will seek the warmest water. It will not be in the shallow parts of the lake. It will be in the deeper water, 15 to 30 feet deep in most lakes. If you know a place in that depth with structure that will be best. The shallow areas of the lake will not have enough oxygen either.

Ice fishing for crappies has advantages over open water fishing. The fish will school tighter and will be easier to find. They have fewer places where they can have comfort in winter. They will more often be in larger schools and suspended over deeper water.

You will need to drill holes to find the fish. You can tell kind of where the fish will be if you do your homework, but once you get to the lake, you will need to drill to find them. Therefore, some of the main tools for effective ice fishing are a good auger and a portable fish finder.

Another handy tool if you cannot afford a flasher is a small depth finder, so you can drop the sensor in the hole to see structure and depth. There are several of them on the market. Several of them work through an app you get on your phone, so they are inexpensive and are handy to have. They are also extremely helpful when ice fishing.

Another technique for finding fish is one you do not want to ignore. Where is everyone else fishing? You can strike out on your own to find fish, but that will take work drilling and using your locator to find them. One hole is also not enough. You should go to and area you think fish are and drill four of five holes around the area and look for fish on the locator. A few feet in depth will matter when looking for a school of crappies.

If your crappie fishing and you catch a bluegill, drop the bait down 5 to 10 feet. Crappies will suspend under a school of bluegills if they can.

The best times of the day are late morning into early afternoon.

In deeper impoundment lakes the crappies will move along channels and other contours in deeper water.

You want to use ultralight tackle and shorter rods for ice fishing for crappies. A light spin-casting reel is best. Spool it with 4-pound line. A line counter can also be helpful when ice fishing. You will always be vertical fishing with small baits.

Sometimes the strikes in the winter are light.

For live bait, the best options are wax worms, and maggots.

Use small ice jigs. You can tip them with a minnow, wax worm, or maggots. When you do vertical jigging with ice jigs, move the jig up and down only an inch or two at a time. The fish are kind of sluggish in the cold water; they do not want to move much or fast.

White, yellow, and chartreuse are the best colors year-round. Even more so in the winter.

Small jigs in winter are best. 1/64 oz to 1/16 oz jigs. The most popular ice fishing jigs are teardrop jigs. You can get them in many colors and made of lead or tungsten. The tungsten jigs are better, but they are much more expensive. **[Here is a nice set of non-tungsten ones on Amazon for a good price.](#)**

[Here are some nice tungsten teardrop jigs on Amazon.](#)

Tip the jigs with wax worms, maggots, a minnow, or a plastic body. The Berkley Gulp minnows can also be highly effective through the ice. **[Here are the perfect ones](#)** for crappie fishing.

A Swedish pimple jig is another popular and effective winter jig. Tip this with maggots or waxworms.

Most places you may use over one line when ice fishing. This makes it easy to set up one line with a bobber and a good lively minnow, and then jig with the other line.

EATING CRAPPIES

As far as taking fish to eat, it is tough to beat crappies. The meat is a good firm white meat. They also are easy to fillet quick with no bones. When you fry them, you get crisp cooked fillets that taste great.

There are many ways you can prepare crappies. Like any other white meat fish, one of the best ways is to fry it in butter. I like to use shore lunch for the covering and fry them in a cast-iron skillet on the stove in melted butter. So good.

Minnesota has low daily limits compared to some states, but you can still get enough for a good meal. Minnesota has some of the lowest limits and limits on how many rods you can use per person. The reason is the shorter growing season limits the number and size of fish. [Here is a link to the regulations](#) on crappies in the lower 48 states.

CONCLUSION

Crappie fishing is popular and growing in popularity every year. The reasons are obvious if you have done it. It is fun and yet a challenge at the same time. You can go out one day and catch a boatload of fish, then go to the same place the next day and catch none. Knowing why that happens is what is the difference between you being a fisherman or a great fisherman.

Knowing the tips in this book and putting them to use in your everyday quest to catch more crappies, will help you become a better fisherman and will make your fishing experiences more enjoyable, and that is what it is all about.

Fishermen spend hundreds of millions of dollars per year on fishing equipment and lures and boats to help them be a better fisherman, but the key to being the best you can be, is knowledge and being able to act on the knowledge you have.

Thanks for downloading and reading my book. Reviews are important to getting more exposure and getting the knowledge to more people. Please [go to the site and leave](#) a review on the book. Thank you.

I have a fishing newsletter I will keep you informed about new techniques, new equipment, and thing about freshwater fishing. Sign up it here today.

ABOUT ME

My name is Steve Pease. I live in the Northern suburbs of the Twin Cities in Minnesota.

I have been writing for about six years. I have written several hundred articles for Hub Pages and for examiner over the years. For Examiner I wrote a column for the Twin Cities on Disc golf, and one on Cycling in the Twin Cities, and one on Exercise and fitness for the Twin cities.

I write on subjects I am passionate about, disc golf, exercise, photography, cycling, fishing, and topics that deal with Christian beliefs.

My father is a retired minister, and he has written many books. I have edited many of them and have them available on my site that cover many topics of interest to Christians today. I have also written an Old Testament trivia book on my own.

I have been playing disc golf since 1978 and love the sport. The greatest thing about disc golf is at age fifty-eight I am still competitive and beat players much younger than me. Disc golf is a sport you can play at almost any age if you can walk.

I have taken several hundred thousand pictures over the last 35 years and I am always trying to improve my photography. My goal is always to take the best shots I can. I want people to say wow when they look at my shots. I went through the photography course at New York Institute of photography many years ago. What I learned from the course and my years of experience was worth every dollar.

The key to be a great photographer is to see things that most people do not see, or in a way they did not see it. My favorite types of photography are landscape, portrait, animals and infrared. I have shot several weddings and spend hundreds of hours just exploring different places looking for great things to take pictures of.

I have been an avid fisherman since I was a kid. I have had 2 bass fishing boats over the years, but I enjoy fishing for my kayak. I have a sit inside old town kayak, and a sit on top feelfree Moken 12 fishing kayak. I also have two old town canoes for going to the boundary waters wilderness area or just paddling around lakes in my area.

The hardest part about fishing from a kayak is trying to decide what not to take with me. As with most bass fishermen I have tons of equipment, and I always feel I need to take it all with me, just in case. Kayak fishing has made me downsize just to make everything fit in my kayak.

I spend most of my fishing time catching bass and northern pike. But if I am looking for a good meal, you can beat crappies and sunfish. I have spent most of my time fishing freshwater, but I have caught saltwater fish. The biggest was a 380-pound bull shark off Key West Florida in 1985.

I have also loved biking and exercising since I was in my early teens. I like to read nonfiction book so I can keep learning new things all the time. Many of the things I learn I want to share with you and help enrich your life. I want to pass on the knowledge I have learned over the years and share it with others.

Thanks again

Check out my book site for other good books.
Stevepease. net

OTHER BOOKS YOU MAY BE INTERESTED IN

Bass fishing boxed set
My 5 books to help you catch more bass

Do you want to know how to go on a new lake and catch bass like you fish it all the time? One of the toughest things for weekend Bass fisherman is knowing where to find fish. The problem comes when you fish a lake you have not fished before. Without the experience, you do not know where to fish unless you have a plan.

Kayak fishing, how to get started and set up your boat

Kayak fishing is growing in popularity by leaps and bounds for many good reasons. Most of the reasons for the popularity are practical reasons that make sense.

Northern Pike Fishing

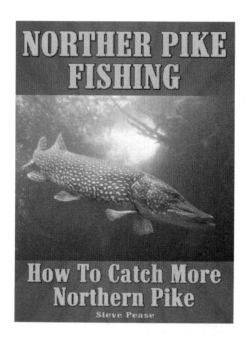

Why you should read this book

This book does not cover every aspect of Pike fishing. I wrote this book so you can take it with you or read it the night before hitting the water. This is so you can have all the best tips and techniques fresh in your mind. It an easy read which will help you remember all the best ways to catch Pike when you get in the boat.

I read a saying that makes me think of catching Pike. It said, "God let me catch a fish today so big that when I talk about it later, I don't even have to exaggerate its size." This is a possibility when fishing for Pike almost anywhere they roam. Every cast you throw in Pike waters could get you hooked on the biggest freshwater fish you will ever catch.

Made in the USA
Columbia, SC
29 May 2025

58625204R00041